This book belongs to:

Name: _____

Date: _____

Contact: _____

_____

Cover art: Pastel by Adhav Dhanavel Kumar, 10.
Published in *Stone Soup* Magazine, February, 2018.

Stone Soup, founded in 1973, is published by Children's Art Foundation—Stone Soup Inc., a nonprofit organization based in the Unted States. Find out more at Stonesoup.com.

www.ingramcontent.com/pod-product-compliance
Lightning Source LLC
Chambersburg PA
CBHW022016290426
44109CB00015B/1189